Original title:
The Apple's Heart

Copyright © 2025 Creative Arts Management OÜ
All rights reserved.

Author: Giselle Montgomery
ISBN HARDBACK: 978-1-80586-267-3
ISBN PAPERBACK: 978-1-80586-739-5

Orchard's Hidden Embrace

In a grove where laughter sways,
Fruits wear smiles on sunny days.
Wobbling branches, giggling pears,
Bouncing apples with silly flares.

When the wind begins to tease,
Orchard critters dance with ease.
Squirrels in tiny top hats prance,
While rabbits join the playful dance.

Beneath the leaves, they tell a joke,
A quirky fruit in every poke.
Cider barrels buzz with glee,
As bubbling laughter fills the spree.

In this orchard, joy runs wild,
Each fruit behaving like a child.
Just a nibble brings delight,
In this hidden world, so bright!

Beneath the Skin

A red delight, round and bright,
Twirls in the breeze, quite a sight.
With a crunch, it plays a tune,
Bouncing 'round like a goofy loon.

Beneath the skin, secrets hide,
Sweet whispers of joy, what a ride!
Teeth dive in, oh what a mess,
Juices dribble - pure happiness!

Harvest Moon's Call

Under the glow of the big, round moon,
Fruits giggle, joining the tune.
Swinging on branches, they joke and tease,
Tickling the wind with their playful breeze.

Farmers chuckle, baskets in tow,
Collecting laughs where the silly winds blow.
With each pluck, a chuckle shared,
Nature's humor - unapologetically bared!

Crimson Core

Once a seed with dreams to soar,
Now in a lunchbox, waiting for more.
Telling tales to the cheese and bread,
Of all the fun that it once had.

With a grin, it shows its core,
"Who knew being snacked on would be such a score?"
In the lunchroom, its laughter spreads,
A fruity prankster, it fills our heads!

Seeds of Longing

Little seeds with dreams so grand,
Plotting adventures across the land.
They giggle and wiggle, wanting to grow,
"Let's be a tree and steal the show!"

In a garden, they make a fuss,
Reaching for sunlight, who needs a bus?
Their wishes take flight, with a wink and cheer,
"Oh to be fruit, that's the life, my dear!"

Heartstrings of the Tree

In a garden where critters play,
A plump red fruit has a lot to say.
With a giggle, it rolls down the hill,
Chasing its friends with a fruity thrill.

A worm with a wink climbs aboard,
Singing sweet tunes of being adored.
The leaves shake with laughter so bright,
As the sun tickles all with its light.

Threads of Juiciness

Bouncing and jiggling, what a sight,
These tiny seeds dance with delight.
They spin tales of summer's domain,
While bugs do a jig, never in vain.

In the orchard, folks munch with glee,
Sipping the nectar as happy as can be.
But watch your bite! A splash, a squirt,
Fruit juice fights back, it's all just a flirt.

Sweet Laboratory

In a lab where the green stems mingle,
Scientists taste, mix, and tingle.
They declare, "This one's got zing!"
As the fruits laugh and begin to sing.

A beaker slips, it spills and splats,
Sticky hands wave like happy rats.
With flavors clockwise and upside-down,
Joyful chaos spreads all around.

Pulp of Affection

Oh, the mushy stuff, how it booms!
Smooches and hugs in the fruit-filled rooms.
With blushing peels in flirty attire,
They flirt with the bees, oh what a choir!

And when they meet on a picnic blanket,
It's pure comedy, slicing the fruit like a banquet.
For laughter is sweetest when shared in a bite,
With seeds of humor flying, oh what a sight!

Tantalizing Flesh

In the orchards where the laughter grows,
Fruits wear smiles, dealing playful blows.
A bite reveals a secret sweet,
Who knew that juice could dance on feet?

Bobbing bobbing, the fruit flies high,
Cats and dogs all whistle, oh my!
Juicy jokes in peels so bright,
A snack attack brings pure delight!

Pith and Promise

Though pithy lines may seem quite grim,
They cradle joy beneath each whim.
Ode to seeds in funny hats,
A punchline that has everyone spats!

Promise wrapped in skin so thin,
Roll the dice, let the fun begin!
With every nibble, laughter ignites,
A comedy show in our bites!

Hidden Whispers

In the orchard's shade, secrets prance,
Whispers between the leaves advance.
"Who's the core?" one cheeky berry scoffs,
While the shy apricot just coughs.

Giggles swirl on the gentle breeze,
Tickling boughs and wobbling knees.
Each fruit has tales that make us grin,
They're all in on the juicy spin!

Love's Juicy Center

Beneath the skin, there's love abound,
In every bite, sweet giggles found.
Romance brewed in an orchard's glow,
Where hearts go wandering to and fro.

Dancing seeds in a saucy line,
Finding love in a twist of vine.
Each drop of nectar tells a tale,
Of silly romances that never fail!

The Warmth Within

In a garden bright with cheer,
A fruit shook off its fear.
It rolled away, quite sprightly,
Chasing bees with glee, so lightly.

With a wink, it took a chance,
Inviting birds to join the dance.
Its laughter echoed through the night,
Making shadows take flight.

Harvesting Echoes

A giggling bunch on the vine,
Swayed to a melody, just divine.
When the farmer came by in haste,
They whispered secrets with good taste.

Pies were planned, a feast galore,
But one rolled off, seeking more.
With a plop, it landed on a shoe,
Said, "How's it going? Just passing through!"

Essence of Enchantment

Beneath a tree with a fuzzy grin,
A curious crowd would always spin.
With each bite, a giggle flew,
Of jokes wrapped in a fruity stew.

One claimed wisdom, grassy and bright,
But a worm said, "No, I'm out of sight!"
Together they laughed, a jolly crew,
Chasing dreams with a zingy view.

Layers of Desire

A peeler danced with joy untold,
As secrets of sweetness began to unfold.
With every twist, a tale unfurled,
Of juicy fun in a funny world.

Jams that jiggled, meringues that soared,
A cookbook could only be ignored.
In the kitchen, laughter brewed,
As life was flavored and proudly stewed.

Orchard Secrets

In the orchard, fruits conspire,
Whispering tales, they're quite the liars.
Peaches think they're the star of the show,
While pears prance around, putting on a glow.

Grapes giggle softly, hanging in bunches,
Trading sweet secrets during their crunchy munches.
'Don't tell the folks, we're the best,' they boast,
As squirrels plan big feasts, it's them they toast.

Juice of Memory

I once knew a fruit with stories to tell,
A tale of "Oops!" that fits just so well.
It rolled off the counter, bounced on the floor,
And splashed on the dog – oh, what a roar!

Tomatoes blushed at the colorful splash,
While lemons joked, 'That was some crash!'
In the blender of life, memories swirl,
Bananas dance, giving laughter a twirl.

Celestial Harvest

In the sky, the fruits take flight,
With clouds as cushions, they zoom at night.
Cherries chase stars, while apples drop tricks,
Sending the moon a few fruity clicks.

Plums gather dust from the Milky Way,
Claiming their space in a fruity ballet.
The cosmos applauds their edible spree,
While comets groan, 'We just want to be free!'

Forbidden Fruit

On a daring tree, the fruit gives a wink,
'Come take a bite! What do you think?'
It whispers sweet nothings, quite contrary,
'Ignore the rules; let's be legendary!'

But every brave soul, just like a knight,
Fell for the charm of that tempting bite.
In the silence that followed, a giggle arose,
As the fruit rolled on, striking a pose!

Lush Reveries

In a garden, fruits do dance,
Whispering secrets, taking a chance.
A wobbly pear took a tilt,
Fell for a grape, in laughter built.

Cherries giggle, plump and bright,
Wishing on leaves under moonlight.
Bananas slip, but still they grin,
Cheering each other, let the fun begin!

Sculpted Flesh

An orange rolled up with a sigh,
Said, "I'm juicier than you, oh my!"
A melon flexed, quite the affair,
"Careful now, don't squash my flair!"

Avocado smug, in creamy guise,
Declared, "I'm guacamole's prize!"
But pineapple laughed, spiky and loud,
"I'm the king, come eat, be proud!"

The Core Connection

Two apples met, both wearing hats,
Swapping jokes about the bats.
One said, "I'm crisp and so refined!"
The other winked, "Let's peel the rind!"

Jokes flew like seeds in the breeze,
Turning frowns into giggling wheezes.
A seedling piped up, 'What's the scoop?'
"Just core jokes, join the fruity troop!"

Radiant Hearts

In a bowl of colors, fun galore,
The fruits debated who's less a bore.
The banana grinned with a cheesy quirk,
"I'm slipping through life, that's my work!"

Peach said, "I'm fuzzy, what's your excuse?"
"I'm smooth and sweet, you better let loose!"
While grapes rolled, all in a ball,
"Let's juice the day, let's have a ball!"

Silken Veins

In a garden bright and spry,
A cheeky fruit caught my eye,
It danced with glee, oh what a show,
With silken veins, it stole the glow.

Its witty skin—a jovial peek,
A playful jibe from a fruity cheek,
It quipped about the autumn breeze,
While spinning tales among the trees.

Round and plump, this jester bold,
Inventing jokes its friends were told,
With every bite a giggle burst,
Delicious laughter was rehearsed.

So when you meet this fruity knave,
Remember laughter—it's the crave!
A bite of joy from nature's patch,
This fruity fun, it's quite the catch!

Tender Core

Inside the fruit, a party brews,
With whispers sweet, and silly news,
A tender core with jests galore,
A curious taste that begs for more.

It dreams of pies and tasty tarts,
With every slice, it plays its parts,
A funny face, a chuckle shared,
In every crunch, its love declared.

When sugar sprinkles light the way,
This little core begins to sway,
With all its friends, it sings in tune,
Beneath the sun, and 'neath the moon.

So take a bite, enjoy the cheer,
For in each core, there's nothing sheer,
A funny tale, no need for lore,
Just sweet delight and giggles galore!

Beneath the Surface

Beneath the skin, a world so bright,
A hidden dance, a joyful sight,
With seeds that plot amusing schemes,
Oh, what a riot! It bursts with dreams.

The surface shines, but wait, don't bite,
For beneath lies such pure delight,
A wriggly laugh, a quippy sigh,
Life's juiciness will make you cry.

With nectar spilled, they start to play,
Imagining roles in a grand ballet,
While laughter tickles through the crowd,
In every crunch, they laugh out loud.

So peel away the fruity guise,
And seek the treasure that underlies,
A giggle burst from nature's spin,
A funny feast that draws you in!

Vibrant Heartstrings

In orchards lush, the strings are drawn,
Vibrant tales with every dawn,
Each pluck a note, a melody,
Of fruity fun and glee—oh me!

The heartstrings hum, a jolly beat,
With jokes and giggles so delightfully sweet,
Though serious fruit sits calm and still,
Its vibrant tune will make you thrill.

With every row of fruity friends,
A symphony of laughter blends,
In tangled roots and leafy schemes,
They jive along in fruity dreams.

So dance along beneath the trees,
Join in the fun, feel that sweet breeze,
For in this grove, with silly sights,
Vibrant strings bring forth delight!

Eden's Legacy

In a garden full of cheer,
A fruit with whispers near,
A bite that brings a grin,
A dance for the brave within.

With a crunch, it's quite the tease,
Each nibble raises knees,
Yet chuckles fill the air,
As juice drips everywhere!

Laughing creatures form a line,
For a taste of sunshine,
Who needs the pot of gold,
When laughter's bright and bold!

Eden's tales of silly fun,
In the shade and sun,
The legacy lives on, you see,
In every bite and giggle—whee!

Vital Essence

A fruit that laughs and shines,
With curves and squishy lines,
A potion for the brave,
That tickles and will save!

Each crunch is a little prank,
With juices in a rank,
A sugary surprise inside,
That makes the giggles collide!

Forget the fancy drinks,
This fruit makes you think,
Could something so divine,
Be a part of your design?

Vital essence of sweet chance,
Makes us leap and dance,
In the orchard, we delight,
With each silly, juicy bite!

Nature's Ruby

In the orchard's shiny glow,
Red treasures start to show,
A berry filled with cheer,
That brings the laughter near.

With a toss into the air,
You're faced with more than flair,
A juicy giggle, oh so bright,
As flavors take their flight!

Nature's gems that bounce and roll,
With mischief as the goal,
Every bite a jolly jest,
This ruby's simply the best!

So gather 'round and share the joke,
As nature's laughter spoke,
It's silly how we crave,
These fruits of fun we save!

Craving the Forbidden

A flash of color, oh so bright,
Calls to mischief, pure delight,
With giggles hiding in disguise,
This tasty trick has clever lies!

It teases from the leafy bed,
With whispers tickling every head,
Craving what we shouldn't touch,
The thrill of wanting oh-so-much!

In shadows, daring hearts will gleam,
For the flavor of a dream,
So come, take a joyous leap,
Into the wild where secrets creep!

Forbidden in its zany ways,
It turns dull moments into plays,
So seek the fun, and never fear,
The laughter's always near!

Echoes of Harvest

In the orchard, fruits do dance,
Giggling lightly, in their prance.
Wobbling on their little stems,
Singing sweetly, teasing gems.

"Pick me first!" the juiciest cries,
While the bruised one just sighs.
A game of tag among the trees,
While squirrels snatch snacks with ease.

Round and round the baskets roll,
Bouncing with laughter, that's the goal.
A mischievous wind joins the fun,
Whirling leaves, oh what a run!

"Who will munch on us tonight?"
All the fruits giggle in twilight.
"Let's hope for pie, sweet and grand,
Or juice galore, just as we planned!"

Secrets of the Orchard

In the hush of leafy waves,
Whispers fly from tree to knave.
"Did you hear about the pear?"
Winks and chuckles fill the air.

Rumors spread like cider bliss,
About a fruity, kisser's kiss.
Tomatoes blushing, in delight,
Squeezed into a salsa fight!

An apple pried with sticky hands,
Schemes of fruit in berry bands.
They plan a party, oh so bold,
Where every snack will soon unfold.

In shadows where the secrets lay,
Fruits giggle and jive all day.
With clever cuts, they dance and twirl,
Beneath the moon, they spin and swirl!

Harvesting Passion

Gather 'round with bags in hand,
Swapping stories, aren't they grand?
"Who will bake with me tonight?"
Arguing over who's just right.

Flour flying, what a sight!
Sifting sugar, pure delight.
Lemon shouts, "Don't forget me!"
While cherries laugh, wild and free.

Mix it up, let's make a mess,
A sprinkle here, a squirt, no less.
Gooey fingers, sticky fun,
Licking spoons when baking's done!

Each bite bloomed with love so sweet,
Muffins bursting with cheer to eat.
Laughter rises with each crumb,
In our kitchen, here we come!

Bitter Truths

The garden whispers secrets old,
Not every tale is sweetly told.
In shadows lie the bruised and sad,
Not all that glitters makes you glad.

A worm crawls in, "I'd like a taste!"
Making some cross, "This isn't waste!"
"I'm crunchy, fresh!" the apple scoffs,
With squishy truth, the bragging's off.

"I'll roll down the hill!" puffs one bold,
But lands with a thud, feeling cold.
"My zest for life was just too grand,
Now I sit lonely in this sand."

Yet laughter echoes in the grove,
For even bruised, they're still beloved.
In every bite, both joy and pain,
Life's funny dance in sunlight and rain.

Orchard Dreams

In a grove where apples sway,
Squirrels plot, they laugh and play.
Wiggling worms join in the fun,
They dream of snacks under the sun.

Branches droop with fruity loads,
The cider's bubbling, laughter explodes.
A peach got jealous, threw a fit,
But in the orchard, all's well, what a hit!

Bumblebees hum a silly tune,
While picking pears, there's room for a boon.
With pies that giggle, here we stand,
To feast with laughter, all hand in hand.

Fruits wearing hats, that's the scene!
The juiciest gathering you've ever seen.
In this orchard, no one feels blue,
Just fruity dreams and antics anew!

Beneath the Flesh

Under skins so shiny bright,
Lies a crunch that's pure delight.
Seeds are giggling, playing tricks,
In juicy layers, oh what a mix!

Peel back tales of laughs and bites,
Every crunch, a wild invite.
We're fruit's best pals, sharing the zest,
In this fruity banquet, we are blessed!

A pit's mischief, a core's surprise,
Lemon's sour face, oh, how it cries.
But sweetness wins in this salad twist,
Where humor reigns, and no one is missed.

Behind their coats, so bright and bold,
Are stories of joy that must be told.
With every slice, a giggle's found,
Beneath the flesh, laughter's unbound!

Bitter-Sweetness

In the orchard of wit, flavors collide,
Bittersweet jokes, apples in stride.
A cider's laugh is full of cheer,
While grapefruits pout, oh dear, oh dear!

The sweetness winked, the tangy teased,
Fruit salad humor, we all are pleased.
With puns as ripe as orchard's hue,
A cherry on top is the humor stew.

Sour notes clash with sweet delight,
In fruity dances, laughter takes flight.
An apple's grin, a punchline bright,
Together we jam through day and night.

Bitter-sweet laughter fills the air,
Every tart joke, a laugh to share.
In this fruity world, let's all partake,
With humor so juicy, for goodness' sake!

Anatomy of Desire

An apple a day, or so they say,
Brings desire in a fruity way.
Glossy skin and a cheeky grin,
Temptation starts right under our skin.

Oh, the fruit-flirtation, how it sways,
Peaches blush, while lemons play.
With cores exposed and seeds aflight,
This juicy game is pure delight.

Strawberries whisper, "C'mon, join in!"
While cherries giggle, fueled by sin.
In this garden, love's pretty clear,
Fruits have feelings, let's all cheer!

So take a bite, feel the zing,
In this anatomy, laughter's king.
All these fruits, in one silly role,
Bringing joy to every hungry soul!

Forbidden Delicacy

In the orchard where mischief grows,
A shiny fruit, everyone knows.
With a wink and a giggle, we decide,
To take a bite, can we hide?

Juicy bites with a crunch so loud,
Laughter echoes; we're feeling proud.
Sweet and tart, it's a dance of flair,
Caught snacking by folks unaware.

We juggle with seeds like little clowns,
Splitting our sides instead of towns.
With sticky fingers and grinning teeth,
Our secret's safe—until we breathe!

So nimble we poke, and then we dart,
This fruit of folly, oh so smart!
With every nibble, a joke's in place,
In this orchard, we're winning the race!

Sensual Seedlings

Tiny sprouts with a cheeky grin,
Dancing in rows, let the fun begin!
With sunshine kisses and playful waves,
These baby greens are the giggling knaves!

They stretch and yawn, as if to tease,
Who knew plants could bring such ease?
In their soil beds, they wiggle and play,
Making garden life a wild cabaret!

"Do you think they feel?" we slyly ponder,
As they sway and spin and simply wander.
In this wild plot, we feel so spry,
As nature's jesters beneath the sky!

Each leaf tickles our curious sides,
In this leafy fest, oh how it slides!
With laughter blooming, seedlings cheer,
In this green playground, we have no fear!

The Taste of Temptation

A bite of sin on a vibrant plate,
Just one more taste—it's never too late!
With flavors dancing, a merry jig,
This sweet seduction is rather big!

Flavors mingle like friends at play,
Each morsel whispers, "Stay, oh stay!"
Crisp and sweet, oh what a thrill,
Eating with glee, and it's never still!

Our forks are twirling like ballerinas,
Diving into flavors, what a scene!
Temptation's rhythm makes hearts delight,
As laughter spins through every bite!

This banquet of laughter, so divine,
With every scrumptious bite, we recline.
So let's devour as the sun forgets,
In this joyful feast, no regrets!

Cultivating Yearnings

In the garden of dreams, we plant our wishes,
Watered with laughter and silly blisses.
As sprouts of joy reach for the sky,
We cultivate giggles; oh, my oh my!

Tending to hopes like silly weeds,
Every chuckle's a sprinkle that feeds.
With whimsy gardens, we play each role,
Nurturing banter, nourishing soul!

With each darned bloom, aspirations sprout,
In a patch of humor, there's never doubt!
We harvest laughter; oh what a sight,
In this garden, everything feels right!

So let's sow dreams with a wink and a grin,
In this fertile field, let the fun begin!
As we savor each moment, in chuckles we trust,
In cultivating yearnings, it's simply a must!

Orchard Shadows

In the orchard where laughter flows,
Apples giggle as the breeze blows.
Silly worms dance in their skin,
Dreaming of pies they wish to win.

The trees play hide and seek all day,
Birds join in, chirping away.
A squirrel shimmies, a playful grin,
Chasing dreams on a whimsy spin.

They feign a blush, redder than sin,
As humans gather, indulging within.
But those round fruits just roll their eyes,
To chuckle in silence, oh what a prize!

In this patch of joy, oh what a scene,
Nature's comedy, pure and keen.
With every bite, the chuckles grow,
In the orchard, where humor throws!

Solace in the Flesh

Juicy laughter rings in delight,
As friends munch under the moonlight.
Green skins glimmer, tales unfold,
Of silly fables, bold and old.

The crunch of sweetness brings a cheer,
As seeds scatter, like tiny deer.
A gnome giggles, his hat askew,
Wishing for apples, and maybe a stew!

Each bite a jest, each core a quip,
With every nibble, they take a trip.
To lands where fruit could talk and sing,
And trees wore hats, an odd spring fling.

In this joyous feast, we find our bliss,
A banquet of chuckles, how can we miss?
As flavors mingle, the fun abounds,
In sweetened laughter, life resounds!

Nectar of the Gods

Beneath the boughs of heavenly trees,
Goddesses dance in the buzzing breeze.
With nectar swirling, they take a sip,
Winking at mortals with every flip.

The sunbeams giggle, tickled by dew,
As petals sprinkle a joyful hue.
A clownish bee, with golden eyes,
Mistaken for royalty, claims the prize!

The fruits conspire with a cheeky jest,
Challenging each other to a zest fest.
Their sweetness a spell, delightful and sly,
Every crunch sends giggles soaring high.

With humor mixed in the juicy blend,
Life's simple joys, they always send.
As laughter ripens in nature's land,
Fruitful giggles spread, oh so grand!

The Heart Within

In every fruit, a secret hides,
A tale of giggles the orchard bides.
With mushy interiors, they joke and jest,
Claiming to be nature's very best!

The seeds all gather for a big debate,
Which has the best jokes to circulate?
One cracked a pun about juicy fate,
While another promised to be first rate!

As the winds whisper funny fruity lore,
Trees sway gently, begging for more.
They chuckle and sway, in harmony's groove,
Nature's jesters, always in the mood!

A laughter fest beneath the sun,
Whimsical parties, oh what fun!
In gardens where food and humor combine,
Life's ripe laughter grows, intertwined!

Sunkissed Temptations

Oh juicy fruit, so round and bright,
You tease my taste with just one bite.
A crunch that sings, a splash of glee,
You're sweet as pie—just wait and see!

In grocery aisles, you strut your stuff,
With winks and giggles, all the fluff.
I try to choose, but who could dare,
Resist your charm or fruity flair?

With every slice, there's joy and juice,
I'm now convinced—you're my excuse.
To munch and crunch, it feels so right,
A fruit party, all day and night!

So let's embark on this silly spree,
A fruity delight, just you and me.
Let giggles burst with every chew,
At this banquet, oh how we'll stew!

Beneath the Fragile Skin

Peel it back, the fun begins,
With laughter hiding underneath the skins.
Each layer drips with giggling zest,
A fruity joke, I must confess!

In this adventure, we take a ride,
Where puns and pips go side by side.
The crunches echo, a silly tune,
As we laugh and munch, oh what a boon!

Why do you roll off the kitchen counter?
Like a clumsy chef, in a fruit encounter!
You've got the moves, so sweet, so sly,
Rolling away, but I'm not shy!

So here we are, just me and you,
Crafting jokes with every chew.
Underneath your color so bright,
Lies a giggle that's pure delight!

Orchard's Pulse

In an orchard lush, where laughter grows,
Each branch a joke, oh how it shows!
With every rustle, it's clear to see,
This fruity place is where I want to be!

With whimsical thoughts, I climb so high,
To seek the fruit that catches the eye.
The squirrels giggle as they sneak a bite,
To join this party, oh what a sight!

The wind sings tales of fruit and fun,
Around the trees where jokes are spun.
I pluck my treasure, bright and spry,
A juicy gem, oh how I'll fly!

So let's dance 'neath the trees with cheer,
As juicy laughter fills the air.
With every crunch, we'll dance and twirl,
In this orchard's pulse, our joy unfurl!

Flavorful Whispers

In every bite, a secret hides,
A whispered tale that giggles and glides.
Within your skin, sweet stories churn,
With every taste, my heart does yearn!

Oh, you fruity jester of color so bold,
With tales of humor waiting to be told.
With each crunchy peel, a joke takes flight,
Tickling my senses, oh what a delight!

Like bouncing balls of sugary glee,
You roll into my day, oh so carefree.
Join me as we savor and grin,
Each delicious moment, let's dive right in!

So prompt the laughter, let flavors dance,
In this fruity whirl, we'll take a chance.
Together we'll laugh, munch and play,
In flavorful whispers, come what may!

The Crimson Core

In the orchard, a fruit sat bold,
Its stories are juicy, and often told.
With a wink and a smile, it sways,
Every bite's a new game it plays.

Dressed in red, it thinks quite grand,
In a world of fruit, it makes a stand.
"Take a bite, if you dare!" it shouts,
While its friends giggle and twist about.

"Oh, I'm sweet!" it boasts, "Try me, please!"
But watch out for the worms in the trees.
With a squirt and a plop, they lead the chase,
Setting off a comical fruit race!

So here's to the fruit with a mind so bright,
Spreading laughter from morning to night.
In every crunch, there's a tale to share,
Of a cheeky red friend with flair to spare.

Nectar of the Soul

In a garden alive with cheer,
A plucky fruit is drawing near.
With nectar sweet and charm so bold,
It tells tall tales that never grow old.

"Take a sip, it's pure delight!
I'm the secret to feeling right!"
With a giggle, it rolls on the ground,
Chasing dreams where joy is found.

When life gets sour, it takes a chance,
With a squirt of flavor, it sparks a dance.
Beckoning all, it twirls with glee,
Inviting the bugs to join the spree!

So let's raise a toast to this fruity sprite,
That brightens our day and lights up the night.
In every drop, a laugh we'll find,
As it spins through the garden, sweet and kind.

Twilight in the Grove

As twilight settles, the grove comes alive,
With fruits making plans for a big night dive.
"Let's play hide and seek!" one whispers low,
While shadows dance in the evening glow.

A pear giggles loud, "I'll find you first!"
While oranges chuckle, their laughter burst.
Underneath leaves, they shiver and shake,
Mischief brewing by the cool little lake.

"Don't peek!" calls out the berry, so bright,
As they plot the perfect hiding spot right.
With a rustle and shuffle, the fun's about,
As the fruits take off, igniting a rout!

Laughter rings out as dusk fades away,
In this fruity frolic, they dance and they play.
So here's to the twilight, full of cheer,
Where mischief and laughter are always near.

Temptation's Core

In a basket, a round one grins with flair,
"Come closer, my friend, if you dare!"
With allure so sweet, and charm to spare,
It knows how to tempt; it's quite the affair.

"Crunch me, munch me, leave worries behind,
I'm the taste that you've been hoping to find!"
With every bite, it's pure delight,
While nearby fruits share in the silly sight.

When the dinner bell rings, it sings a tune,
Planning its plot under the silver moon.
"Who needs your greens when I'm here to stay?"
It winks at the veggies, pushing them away.

So let's celebrate this charming delight,
With each playful nibble, it feels so right.
In a world filled with fun, and laughter galore,
It brings a chuckle, wishing for more!

Serpent's Offering

A snake with a grin, oh what a tease,
Promising knowledge, as smooth as you please.
He wriggled and squirmed, with charm in his eyes,
But watch out for bites disguised as sweet lies.

In a garden so lush, with colors all bright,
He whispered of truths that would bring you delight.
A crunch from a fruit, oh the promise was grand,
Who knew it could lead to a hiccup so planned?

Now folks in the garden play dodgeball with fate,
Wondering how they could have been so late.
A munch and a crunch, now they dance in a rush,
As the serpent just laughs, oh the fruity hush!

So if you see an apple, just give it a glance,
Ask the snake first, before taking the chance.
For sometimes a gift comes wrapped up with a jest,
And munching on fruit may not always be best.

Embrace of the Orchard

In an orchard so grand, where the trees all sway,
The fruits had a party, shouting "Hey, we play!"
They bounced on their branches, so cheeky and bright,
Inviting the birds for a karaoke night.

The pears with their jiggles, the peaches in rhyme,
All singing and dancing, oh what a time!
While apples just giggled, and rolled 'round the ground,
Playing hide and seek with that big hairy hound.

A cluster of grapes fell with laughter and cheer,
While cherries declared, "We're the best fruit this year!"
With every last bite, brought the laughter anew,
But watch out for seeds, they could get quite the boo!

So join in the fun, let your worries take flight,
In the embrace of the orchard, everything's right.
With humor and fruit, life's a sweet little game,
Just know when you bite, it's not always the same.

Dripping Delight

A juicy red fruit, so shiny and round,
Tells tales of sweetness that's always profound.
But when you take a bite, oh what a surprise,
The juice squirts out, and then right in your eyes!

With fingers all sticky, and laughter in air,
You'll soon find yourself in a fruity affair.
"Who knew such delight could leap out in a splash?"
As you wipe off the nectar, you giggle and dash.

On picnic blankets spread, all munching away,
The snacks turning funny with each fruity play.
A blueberry bounces, oh just what a sight,
While the watermelon rolls with sheer sheer delight!

So gather your fruits, let the fun be your guide,
And don't mind the mess, just enjoy the ride.
For in every sweet bite, there's laughter to share,
In the circus of flavor, you'll find joy everywhere!

Entwined Roots

In a garden so clever, where roots intertwine,
Lived veggies and fruits that made dinner divine.
With carrots so happy, they wiggled with glee,
While tomatoes were calling, "Come dance here with me!"

But apples were jealous, all stuck in their trees,
While the others played games in the warm summer breeze.
"Let's pull us a prank, oh what fun!" they all said,
"Cycle through branches and mess with their heads!"

With laughter and tickles, they swung to and fro,
While the leaves danced around, putting on quite the show.
Down below the soil, the roots shook with mirth,
For even the ground knew the joys of this earth.

So next time you visit, where fruits laugh and play,
Join in the fun, let your worries decay.
For in every sweet moment, and each jolly twist,
Are tales of the garden that simply can't be missed!

Shades of Ripeness

A fruit so round, a vibrant tease,
With colors bright, it aims to please.
But take a bite, oh what a shock,
Juice drips down, it's quite the clock!

Some are green, some are red,
But watch your step, there's goo instead.
When ripe, they burst, a sweet surprise,
Just don't get stuck with sticky pies!

A tree of jokes, oh what a sight,
With branches swaying, oh what a flight.
They laugh and dance in evening light,
While squirrels ponder their next bite!

A chuckle here, a chew on that,
Nature's jesters, fat and flat.
Their humor lies in every crunch,
So grab one quick, let's all have lunch!

The Sound of Crunch

In the orchard, hear it loud,
A crunch so crisp, it draws a crowd.
Bite into laughter, free and wild,
Every munch, a giggling child.

Squeaking squirrels in secret stunts,
Bouncing apples, silly hunts.
A rolling fruit, oh what a show,
Each loud snap makes spirits glow!

Fall leaves dance, and giggles soar,
When apples tumble, they want more.
Ripe and round, they tumble down,
Wearing nature's silly crown!

So gather round the orchard's glee,
With crunchy bites, we laugh with spree.
A sound so sweet, an apple's joke,
As laughter bursts, we all revoke!

Whispers in the Grove

In leafy hideouts, secrets dwell,
With witty tales, the apples tell.
Gossip flows from branch to branch,
As squirrels plot their funny chance.

"Who's stealing shine?" they tease and chuckle,
As sunlight winks, they burst their buckle.
Teasing rivals, red and green,
"Who's the sweetest? Let's make a scene!"

Frolicsome winds bring news and cheer,
Of frosty nights and summer near.
Each swaying branch, a jokester's song,
With whispers soft, they can't go wrong!

So in this grove, let laughter rise,
A fruity jest beneath the skies.
With every breath, a joke on cue,
The apple's tale is fresh and new!

Nature's Temptation

Oh what a sight, a fruit-filled stand,
A tempting feast, all crisp and grand.
With smiles wide, they call us near,
Promising bites of joy and cheer.

"How about a slice?" the apples plead,
"Just one more taste is all you need!"
But watch your step, they start to roll,
On silly missions, that's their goal!

Bouncing high, they laugh and tease,
A fruity riddle carried by the breeze.
"Pick us up, come take a chance,
Join our merry apple dance!"

In nature's pot, they stir the fun,
With every nibble, there's more to shun.
So grab a bunch, let laughter sway,
In nature's game, we laugh and play!

Sweet Morsels of Memory

In a garden where laughter grows,
With critters nibbling on their toes.
A juicy fruit, so round and bright,
Claims to be the star of the night.

Its zingy taste, a joke in disguise,
As seeds inside hatch tiny spies.
They scout the world for a tasty bite,
And giggle at each juicy fight.

One took a dive, thought it could swim,
In a puddle of juice, quite the whim.
The others laughed, oh, such a scene,
As it splashed about with its shiny sheen.

So pick a fruit and join the fun,
With each sweet morsel, smiles begun.
In this orchard's playful, silly spree,
Who knew fruit could bring such glee?

Flesh and Folly

Two fruits sat perched on a high, green pane,
Discussing life, from sunshine to rain.
One was salty, the other sweet,
Together they made quite a juicy treat.

They argued who was the fairest in sight,
The red one said, "I'm the true delight!"
The green one chuckled, with zest and flair,
"But I've got crunch, you've got only air!"

Off came a bite, with a giddy hiss,
Flesh and folly in a juicy bliss.
The pit rolled away, a rogue on a spree,
To join in the laughter, wild and free.

So here's to the fruits with their quirks and charms,
And the silly troubles that come with farms.
For when they unite, what a riot it makes,
In the collision of taste, everyone quakes!

Bittersweet Reverie

Once in a basket, there dwelt a round crew,
A mix of the vibrant, that glowed bright and blue.
They dreamed of a feast, held under the stars,
But one thought the moon tasted just like guitars.

With a giggle and squish, they plotted their paths,
Two rascals conspired to dodge the farmers' wrath.
"Let's roll down the hill and make a grand splash!"
And landed in yogurt, what a fruity mash!

The night grew wild, as they danced in delight,
With each punchy bop, they took off in flight.
"Who knew tangy dreams could tickle so right?"
The orchard erupted in laughter that night.

So treasure your bites, both sweet and the tart,
For laughter and juice are the true works of art.
In a world of mischief, with joy in the air,
We nibble on memories, light as a pear!

Sins of the Orchard

In an orchard where merriment took a stand,
Resided a crew who were quite underhand.
They snuck through the rows, with giggles in tow,
And tasted the blooms—oh, the ruckus did grow!

The elder tree sighed, "What are you up to?"
"Just nibbles and giggles, nothing for you!"
Ripe fruits rolled over, with grins on their skins,
As seeds chuckled softly, delighted by sins.

A ripe berry got stuck on the branch,
Flushed with embarrassment, oh what a dance!
The gang burst out laughing, held onto their sides,
As the fruit swung free on a summer's joy ride.

So beware of the nectar that draws you near,
For in every bite, there's a hint of good cheer.
The orchard's our playground, our laughter, the prize,
In this shady realm, let carefree fun rise!

Deep Within Orchard Souls

In a tree, a secret so sweet,
A fruit that dances on deceit.
With a wink, it calls my name,
In this game of juicy fame.

Branches sway, a playful tease,
Beneath the leaves, a mischievous breeze.
Fruits giggle, they can't keep still,
Hiding their charm with a cheeky thrill.

Ripened dreams all set to pluck,
No need for luck, just a little buck.
But watch your back, the worms conspire,
In this juicy realm, beware their fire.

With every crunch, a chorus sings,
Of orchard joy and silly things.
So take a bite and join the fun,
In this heart, we all are one.

Forbidden Allure

Oh, the color, so bold and bright,
Temptation grows with morning light.
A single bite, what could it bring?
An apple's song, oh, how we sing!

Under branches, we plot and scheme,
Of juicy bites and sweet, wild dreams.
But here's the twist: oh, what a joke,
The laughter spills as secrets broke.

Silly stares from the watchful crow,
Peeking at all the things we sow.
In this orchard of winks and grins,
Where mischief grows and laughter spins.

A daring nibble, hearts in a flutter,
Watch as the juice makes a splash and splutter.
With each glance back at old, wise trees,
Their juicy laughter carried by the breeze.

An Invitation to Indulgence

Gather 'round, my foodie friends,
In this orchard, joy never ends.
With every crunch, let worries cease,
A juicy morsel, a slice of peace.

A round invitation, come take a seat,
Where laughter lives and flavors meet.
With spoons and forks, let chaos reign,
In this feast, there's so much to gain.

Peel back layers of delight in sight,
Colors burst, creating pure light.
Juicy jests on every plate,
In this orchard, we celebrate fate!

Unwrap the giggles, take a huge bite,
A sweet explosion, sheer delight.
So grab a friend and join the rave,
In this orchard, we're all brave.

The Glistening Core

Shining bright, a tempting prize,
With a twinkle, it catches the eyes.
Under sunlight, it plays so coy,
Crafting smiles, a cheeky ploy.

Inside, a surprise, colors collide,
A ribbon of flavors, let's take a ride.
With silly bites, the laughter erupts,
In this core, funny mischief interrupts.

Chomping down, the giggle ascends,
As seeds of joy are scattered like friends.
So, come and savor the silvery glow,
In this orchard, let happiness flow!

Another crunch and the laughs expand,
In this fruity tale, let's take a stand.
So raise your apple, let's cheer galore,
For in laughter, we'll all explore!

Essence of Orchard Dreams

In a garden where fruit thieves roam,
An apple fell, far from its home.
It landed with a comedic thud,
Creating quite the juicy flood.

The worms all giggled, what a sight,
As juice sprayed out in pure delight.
They danced around the shiny skin,
Saying, "Let the apple games begin!"

A breeze blew by with a cheeky grin,
Saying, "Let the apple antics spin!"
The branches shook with laughter loud,
As fruits fell down like nature's crowd.

So here in orchards, dreams take flight,
With apples joking, full of light.
The laughs come rolling like the day,
In this fruity, funny, fanciful play.

Whispering Flesh

A fruit so shiny, red and round,
Hides secrets in its sweet background.
It tickles ribs with every bite,
Whispering jokes late in the night.

Beneath the skin, a giggle grows,
Its juicy punch, a comic show.
Each slice reveals a funny face,
Making sure we're in our place.

With every crunch, we burst with glee,
This fruit's a prankster, can't you see?
It rolls away when you reach near,
Shouting, "Catch me, if you dare, my dear!"

So take a bite, let laughter bloom,
In every bite, there's room for boom!
With whispering flesh, we can't avoid,
The funny ways this fruit will toy.

Sweet Temptation

Oh, sweet temptation, red and round,
You tease us all upon the ground.
A wiggly worm, he takes a seat,
Saying, "This fruit is quite a treat!"

As we reach out, you roll away,
Laughing softly, "Not today!"
You dangle from the leafy bough,
With all your charms, oh, take a bow!

Every bite brings giggles bright,
A sweetness that feels just right.
A maraschino cherry on top,
Making us never want to stop.

In the orchard where chuckles flow,
The sweet temptation steals the show.
With every crunch, the laughter swells,
This fruit's the king of all the spells.

Core of Enchantment

Inside the core, a story spins,
Of juicy battles and cheeky wins.
A fruit that's crafty, with a plot,
In a world where humor is the lot.

With every nibble, charms arise,
Making mouths giggle, big surprise!
The seeds all whisper jokes they know,
As we munch down, they steal the show.

So gather round for this tasty treat,
That bounces, giggles, never beats.
Bursting laughter with every bite,
This core brings joy, pure delight.

In each slice, the magic's clear,
An enchanting fruit that we revere.
So take a chance, give it a try,
With every laugh, we'll reach for the sky!

Forbidden Fruit Reverie

In a garden lush and bright,
A snack that feels just right.
Flavors tempting every bite,
A twist of fate, oh what a sight!

A worm, in dreams, I hear him say,
"Don't munch me, friend, I'm here to play!"
A nibble here, a crunch, hooray!
In this feast, we laugh all day!

The taste is sweet, the juice runs free,
I share a chunk with Big Bee Dee.
"Let's savor this in harmony!"
With giggles buzzing merrily.

So let's indulge, no need to pout,
Especially when crumbs are all about.
A fruity dance, let out a shout,
For playful snacks, there's never doubt!

Harvest of Longing

In orchards bright, I spy a gem,
Dancing daintily on a stem.
My appetite is like a dream,
With thoughts of ripeness bursting at the seam!

Oh, pluck me quick, my heart will race,
With cheeks red-hued, a gleeful face.
Yet nature plays a fleeting chase,
A tug-of-war, a jolly space!

Imagining bites that make me grin,
While sneaky squirrels plot their win.
"Hey, that's mine!" "Oh, where you been?"
Chasing joy, it's all a din!

So feast and frolic in this spree,
With silly jokes beneath the tree.
Each crunch and munch, a grand decree,
Where smiles ripple playfully!

Juicy Echoes

There's a sound, a tempting squish,
Of fruity dreams and blissful wish.
I chase it down with every swish,
A giggle-thrift, oh what a dish!

In shadows cast, a game of tease,
"Catch me if you can," with such ease.
A berry burst, a laugh that frees,
Swiping joy with each bright breeze!

With friends around, I munch away,
Each giggle sweetens the buffet.
Secrets shared in bright display,
Echoes of joy, a jolly play!

So let's not fret or hide our cheer,
Let's roll in laughter, it's crystal clear!
Juicy fun, stay close, my dear,
For fruity frolics, we hold near!

Essence of Eden

In a leafy spot, a wish fulfilled,
Where bright delights make hearts thrilled.
Curious creatures, joy distilled,
In flavors fierce, oh so skilled!

A kingdom ripe, where taste buds dance,
With every crunch, a wild prance.
Sipping sunshine, a chance romance,
Twisting tales in fruity chance!

The laughter pours like nectar sweet,
As buggy buddies huddle to greet.
A playful chase, a fun conceit,
With every bite, we find our feat!

So gather round, let's sing and sway,
In this fruity world, we'll frolic and play.
With chuckles shared, we'll find our way,
To joy that blooms in endless array!

Orchard Whispers

In the orchard where fruits giggle,
A rogue wind gives them a wiggle.
The trees gossip with each sway,
Telling secrets in a funny way.

The sun takes a peek, quite bold,
As shadows dance in marigold.
A worm with dreams of being round,
Spins tales of treasures in the ground.

A squirrel debates with a bee,
Who'll claim the juiciest spree?
They wager nuts by the bushel,
While the flowers blush and squish'll.

With laughter ripe, they share the day,
As leaves join in the silly play.
Who knew a farm could be so loud?
Fruits cheer, "We're the topmost crowd!"

Seed of Red Desires

Once a seed thought it could soar,
Dreamed of places others adore.
It wished on stars, ripe and sweet,
And wanted to dance on everyone's feet.

A gnome said, "You're brave, old chap!"
"Just wait till you take this nap."
The seedlet snoozed under a sun,
Woke up feeling round and fun!

With each roll, it had a blast,
Felt the love that's unsurpassed.
Joined a party with other seeds,
Setting off on laughter's leads.

They giggled through tunnels of dirt,
Beneath the sun, they'd never hurt.
Dreams brewed in every shiny guise,
Oh, the folly of red desires!

Core of Sweet Temptation

In a kitchen, a fruit stands proud,
With glistening skin, it screams out loud.
"Slice me open, see my charm,
I promise you, I won't cause harm!"

Upon the counter, the knife awaits,
"Be gentle now, I've got my mates!"
Peeling off layers, it starts to grin,
"Look at me, a treat from within!"

A cookie whispers from nearby,
"You think you're cool? I just might fly!"
Sugary dreams with a fruity twist,
"Oh no, dear fruit, you'll be missed!"

So they baked and they laughed a lot,
Creating flavors, hilarity hot.
In the oven, a sweet rebellion,
The core became quite a sensation!

Crimson Secrets

In a garden where secrets creep,
Leaves giggle while the roots do leap.
A baby fruit grins from the vine,
"I've got tales that are simply divine!"

Beneath the soil, the funny bugs,
Share whispers of love, and warm hugs.
A ladybug flirts with a bumblebee,
"Will you take me to the peach pit spree?"

The wind carries laughter high,
As petals swirl and nearby fry.
A crimson fruit, full of winks,
Points to the pond where a frog drinks.

They toast with water, joy on display,
Under the sun, they frolic and play.
With crimson secrets, they share delight,
In the garden, all feels just right!

Cradle of Flavor

In a tree with a grin, oh so wide,
Hangs a fruit that can't hide its pride.
Juicy tales in the breeze,
Whisper sweet nothings with ease.

Round and red, the jesters stay,
In the orchard, they dance and play.
With every bite, laughter erupts,
As the squirrels perform their hiccuped hops.

On picnic blankets, they delight,
Creating snacks that feel just right.
Pie and crumble, what a scene,
Life's a feast from these fruits, so keen!

So here's to the fruit that brings cheer,
Witty whispers for all who are near.
It's a party wherever they roll,
Nature's jesters, feeding the soul!

Nature's Bounty

In the garden, don't you know,
The fruits have a theatrical show.
Each bites pops with a giggle,
Flavor bombs that make you wiggle.

Peeling back layers, what a surprise,
Every crunch opens new skies.
Fruits in hats and socks too bright,
Nature's feast, a comical sight!

Swinging from branches, they jive,
In the sun, they feel so alive.
With every munch, a new act starts,
Caught in joy, they conquer hearts.

As we share this merry delight,
Let's toast to the bites divine tonight.
For in every slice, we discover,
Giggles that make the whole world shudder!

The Core of Desire

Nestled tight in a hidden fold,
Lies a treasure, bright and bold.
With a crunch, it spins a tale,
Of sweetness bound to prevail.

Oh, the longing, what a dance,
Nature's flirt, it takes a chance.
With some cheese or chocolate, please,
It's a rendezvous that aims to tease!

Nibbles and bites, a wild affair,
Each flavor's a joke, with laughter to share.
Tickling taste buds with every grace,
A fruit that knows how to embrace.

So slice it up, don't hold back,
Join the fun on this tasty track.
For every munch is a chance to jest,
In this juicy game, we're truly blessed!

Garden of Secrets

In this garden, whispers abound,
Fruits are plotting, oh what a sound!
Under leaves, they giggle and scheme,
Crafting flavors, living the dream.

With every pluck, a chuckle bursts,
Sweet juices flow, satisfying thirsts.
In this patch, they plan their event,
A fruity fiesta, wherever they went!

Hiding tricks in every core,
Beneath their shining, juicy door.
What magic lies in this delight?
With laughter and flavor, everything's right!

To the picnic, they'll journey far,
Each bite a secret, a shining star.
So join the fun, take a chance,
In this garden, fruits love to dance!